# Man I Hate Church

## But I Really Do Love the Lord

Susan Horton

authorHOUSE®

*AuthorHouse™*
*1663 Liberty Drive*
*Bloomington, IN 47403*
*www.authorhouse.com*
*Phone: 1-800-839-8640*



*Published by AuthorHouse 2/28/2012*

*ISBN: 978-1-4678-6994-2 (e)*
*ISBN: 978-1-4678-6995-9 (sc)*

# Foreword

I want to offer a disclaimer about the next chapter in my book collection. There will be some who will take offense to what I am about to say, but then it is supposed to cause some agitation. That is what cultivation is, a stirring. This is not a tell all book to make any one feel bad or blame anyone for what God put in my path to elevate me to the next level in him, but it is a chance to let those of you who have endured "Church" hurt or who is possibly still experiencing the let down of following a "man" of God know you are not alone.

Organized religion has been successful at three things:

1. Distracting us from a true relationship with God and turned us to worshipping man

2. Getting us to doubt our own spiritual intuition and rely on another's

3. Causing us to live in constant fear of damnation by loading us down with unnecessary regulations.

These unnecessary yokes are all outward attempts to placate inward cleanliness. This brings us back to searching for a spirituality that is already in motion. If you are finding it difficult to live the Christian walk, check to make sure you are following the Christ and not the anti-Christ. In order for the tricks of churchliness to work there has to be a belief of necessity.

For instance a man who wants to maintain control of his flock will misuse that scripture that talks about the good shepherd, and put himself in the role of the good shepherd. This friend is the anti-Christ. Jesus Christ is the only shepherd. We are all sheep. We are all in His hands. God has not yet given one man charge over another. Over animals, the birds of the air, even over the plants in the field, but He has never given man charge over another soul.

All souls are mine saith the Lord, and the soul that sinneth it shall die. Let's talk about sin for a second. Sin is defined as estrangement from God. The only thing that estranges us from God is unforgiveness of one another.

The bible explicitly lays out in the form of the Ten Commandments a blue print of a don't list that we all must follow. If we obey all of these and love our neighbor as ourselves, we are in good standing with God, therefore keeping our estrangement to a minimum. Any action that goes against the Ten Commandments is a sin. Jesus bid us to come unto him and he would give us rest; for his burden is easy and his yoke is light. All of these other bands of heaviness placed on our shoulders by man is irrelevant and are not causing any offense to God. They are however, breeding mistrust and disloyalty in the hearts of the children of God and causing them to rebel.

Rebellion is the foundation of the first church of Satan. I was watching a program on this organization and one of the priests said that the entire principle of Satanism is rebellion against that which is holy and pure. We have been looking in the wrong direction for too long.

So many churches are caught up in things like speaking in tongues, laying on of hands, and sprinkling holy oil and restricting secular activity. These silly requirements include things like not going to ballgames or to movies. Some religious practices forbid women from wearing pants, makeup, or even swimming in public. In fact some of the most pious will tell you that in order to reach heaven you can't dance and can't smoke, can't do drugs or perform certain sexual acts, even if you are within the confines of marriage. None of these things are sins. Now the chemical ingestion may cause health hazards, and may even contribute to some criminal activity. The alcohol or drugs themselves are not sins, but the illegal activity that they may provoke can be considered sins.

When we take Tylenol for headaches or drink Nyquil for colds then are we sinning? I used to smoke. As long as I was trying to quit to appease man, I had a greater urgency to smoke. My logic did not make any sense. When I realized that it was killing me, I had all the leverage I needed to make a sound decision to quit. My will to live supersedes my desire to appear clean in the eyes of man. It is same concept with the consumption of drugs. Their use and handling are not sins, but they are against the laws of the land, and God requires us to obey the laws of the land along with keeping his commandments.

Drinking is not a sin. Jesus' first miracle was turning water into wine at a wedding. There are several references to wine in the New Testament. Forbidding the drinking strong drink mentioned in the Old Testament, but that was a requirement for Levites in training. They needed to maintain clarity of thought.

Most of the regulations placed on modern day Christians are done to appear more righteous than we actually are. "All have sinned and fallen short of the glory of God" This implicates that even on our best day our righteousness is as a filthy rag.

As for secular activities we should all be careful of what we are introducing our minds to, but there is no condemnation for participating in them. Isolation from secular activity is the mark of the occult. Some media makes us think and would cause a break in the mindless programming of ritualism. Instead we should be paying attention to things that cause us to be estranged from God. Now the works of the flesh are these:

How many times have we traded real spirituality

for traditionalism just to please some crack pot preacher or some derange member of the mother's board. I had one brother tell me that I needed to get under a covering meaning I needed to join a local church to be covered. Again I thought that was the whole reason for Calvary. In essence what he was saying is that Jesus' blood was not enough, and, and that Calvary needed help and it was going to take a man like him to get me to the faith. Do you know how ridiculous he sounded? He did not mean it in jest, but I felt like rebuking him like Jesus did Peter... "get thee behind me Satan!"

Once again, this is the mark of the anti-Christ. The spirit that Jesus rebuked in Peter was one of emotional proportions and false submission. In short, Peter was being a hypocrite and trying to make himself seem more touched than he actually was. He was causing a scene and it was distracting from the point Jesus was trying to tell the disciples regarding Calvary. This is the same spirit that pastors of ill repute try to evoke in God's children by telling them that a mark of God's spirit here on earth is an outward showing of gibberish, convulsing and rolling around on the floor. Silly parishioners will devote themselves to acting out this weird voodoo like gestures and forget the word says they will know that we are Christians by the love we exemplify. Preachers teach the ceremonious delivery of these ritualisms all the while creating a spiritual deficit. This deficit in turn leaves the believer feeling guilty and inadequate. To top off this parody of true spirituality, he will include the need for you to pay your way out of hardship and despair. Jesus taught morality. Now we have ex pimps and illiterate gangsters robbing people by advocating redemption as long as you pay tithes and offerings. To those of you who are reading this please take your 10% and put it in the bank. Let these lying prophets go get a 9 to 5 like the rest of us. Some of you have been brainwashed for so long until you will argue and take offense to me trying to help you to get away from the curse. We have been plagued with man and his religion for so long until we can't conceive of our restoration via Jesus Christ. Calvary already did what they keep telling us God is planning to do. It is already done; per Jesus, it is finished. We are already complete and entire wanting for nothing. Wake up people! Stop giving away your prosperity. They have you so gone, you feel like it is a sin to take care of yourself. They will applaud you for giving up your money so they can live the life you should be and will admonish you to keep believing God will give you a better one for giving the one he has already provided for you to them. Yes it is as stupid as it sounds. Nobody is benefiting from your giving but a bunch of undeserving crooks. These preachers are taking advantage of our weak wills and need for spiritual validation to control us.

My first impression of spirituality was introduced by this little church that sat on a hill in a place called Happy Holla. Those zealots were the comic relief to the world of religion. They were a bunch of spiritual novices who were making it up as they went along. Most of the fear I learned from them were the foundation for my participation in occultism. Fear, self doubt, and longing to be accepted took me places in the world of religion that most were smart enough not to travel. I was victimized by preachers who took the purest part of me, my love for God and used it against me. With this weapon, those greedy dogs ravaged me financially, emotionally, and spiritually. When I would rebel and take a stand against what was blatant exploitation on the preacher's part, I was openly rebuked and called all manner of evil in the presence of others. The other parishioners would be afraid to challenge any hint of irrational thought and that greedy preacher's plan of domination would be complete. That reverential fear that we are supposed to have for God only has now been bestowed on a man. This story is my own personal experience. Those of you, who are mentioned, forgive me if your heart takes offense to the truth, but it must be told.

## Man I Hate Church!

I was coming home by way of Doogle Middle School, which happened to be positioned directly behind my block. There are 5 houses I have to pass before I make it home. 1[st] house belongs to Aunt Ness, an elderly lady who is just like every other old lady you've ever met.

"Hey Aunt Ness!" I chirp as I pass, but I notice a small garter snake under her porch. I don't panic, but I speed up my pace.

Next house I approach is the Nextons. They are an emaciated bunch whose matriarchal influence is had to deny. In their yard I see a black viper. Before it strikes, I start to run. I am now approaching the steps of a reclusive set of people with as "just us" mentality. In their yard is a king snake. He's more of a visual threat than anything. Then just before I could pass the Steins, I hear the rattle. I pause to try and get my bearings. Which way is he coming from? That was the home of the Pitts. Just like the serpent that guarded their yard, you never knew what was going to come from that house. The father was a letch, the mother had suffered a nervous breakdown, the eldest daughter was a butch; the son was a flighty bubble head and the youngest daughter had a yearning for the buddha. The little pink house in between ours and theirs was vacant so was the yard. Oh but wait, I'm almost home. No, before I could…oh God! This giant king cobra awakes from his nap leaps forward when he sees me and starts slithering wildly towards me. I am so stunned all I can do is scream and shake. This venomous, all consuming reptile was coming to destroy me. Just as he approaches me and prepares to devour me whole, when a chubby dark skinned man falls from the sky and lands directly on its perfectly inflated neck. After he crushes the source of my demise he starts to console me.

As I wake up in a cold sweat, I realize it was just another one of those dreams I have. Sometimes I can see so clearly and other times it's all muddled together. As I rise to go pee, I see the bible on the credenza in the hallway. I always turn to the word of God for solace when things are as bad as they are. I quit school almost a year ago. Shoot the only reason I went in the first place was to please my parents hoping they would for once be proud of me. Needless to say that idea only lasted until the next semester. I was so bogged down in an inferiority complex that I was afraid of everything and I couldn't even enjoy my matriculation as ASU. The only place I went was to the music building. I never ventured outside of that comfort zone. I couldn't tell you what the rest of the campus looked like. My whole life I have been surrounded by spirit breakers. The narrow minded stock that I was bred from made my love for exploration difficult. For anything that was new and exciting was either a sin or just another thing I couldn't do because 'they said so'.

I never knew anything but the confines of my parent's home. They thought they were doing me a favor by locking me away from the rest of the world, but now I know it was case of not knowing how to deal with a child such as myself. I was too much of everything and not enough of anything. This type of sheltering made me socially retarded. Instead of learning how to deal with people, I would avoid them at all cost. I used avoidance as a coping mechanism because I would always say or do something that would end up alienating them; thus making me self conscience and them uneasy. I could start out funny and charming and end up annoying and abrasive.

Perhaps I started to believe what my family thought of me and that was my way of validating it. When I got older, I would use an attitude to make people leave me alone. After a while that was the only way I knew how to behave. I later found out that I was a bipolar dyslexic with a major inferiority complex. Talk about triple pain. If you want to know what it's like to be a bipolar dyslexic, just start driving your car and accelerate to about 75, then as you arc rotating your right foot counter clockwise, rotate your left foot clockwise and make a sharp left turn. Yeah,...I know. That's what it is like for me every day. Now I am 35. Mix that cocktail of confusion with the anguish of being a child. Whew! I am lucky I made it out alive.

Again, because I was an unusual child, it was assumed by the "aints" that my mother made the spiritual gurus of our household that I was demon possessed. Yes folks, I am the demon seed of my family, or so they would have others to believe. You see to keep others from seeing the good in me, my mother would cast this dark light over me making anyone who would take an interest in me believe that I was a demon. This could have been because she never had very much of a child hood herself or it could have been her jealousy of me and over me. I know it is difficult for some of you to believe that a mother could be jealous of her child but mine really was. I know now that a lot of the tormenting I experienced at her and other's hands was because they were jealous of me. I remember this lady at our church that took an interest in me and started buying me clothes and shoes and taking me out to different places, trying to make me into a young woman. This put a stress on the relationship between her and me because up until that moment, my mother had no interest in me what so ever. I remember this fourth of July picnic at the pastor's house where I went barefooted because I didn't have any shoes. There was always some type of wardrobe malfunction; a broken zipper, hems coming unraveled, or ruined stockings. There was no end to this shabby existence in sight. Even if there was a lack of money, there should have been a genuine attempt at teaching and showing me how to be neat with the little I had. To be honest, I believe it was her pleasure to make fun of me.

One Saturday, this lady took me shopping for a Sunday outfit. When I came home, my mother had made a poor attempt at trying to shop for me. She handed me a box with some shoes in it that one of the ladies on our mother board wears. I was glad she was trying, but the look on my face was one of horror and disappointment. Before I knew it she snatched the shoe from me and proceeded to beat me in my head and I could hear my father in the background saying 'that's right'. He was just as bad. He once started an argument with me by putting me down, and then when I began to stick up for myself, he proceeded to punch me with his fists… THEN started yelling for them to bring him a belt. He didn't talk to me for a week. I thought of running away then, but where would I go? Who was going to save me from these two tyrants?

After all they had already told everybody how unruly, hardheaded and disobedient I was. I often wonder what it was about me that made them hate me so much? It wasn't just the clothes, when I started my menses, I was afraid to tell her because I feared getting whipped. I got beaten for everything she could pin on me. I was 15 years old before she stopped spanking me. That last whipping I put up so much of a fight that she had to go take a nap. Then she wakes up with a revelation from the holy ghost that told her she needed to stop whipping me. It got to be the in thing to tell Sister Horton on Susan, and she obliged everyone that had a beef with me. I hate to think that since I wasn't the type you could easily control, these silly impish adults were getting back at me, but what did I know, I was just a child.

There was also the times when I had oppurtunities to go places like Chicago or Birmingham. I had planned to spend the summer with another church member, but my mother sabotaged it by sending word thru my aunt. I was standing right there when she told her that I was real disobedient and her mother is afraid that she will blow up at you. I was helpless to retort. The woman was standing there shocked. I don't know if she was disappointed at me or that my aunt was there bad mouthing me. It wasn't so much that she felt the need to belittle me, but why did she have to make me out to be such a villain? Let's face it I would have gone to Oregon to chop down trees to get away from those two. Later on in life, that same aunt came to me and asked me to forgive her for mistreating me and ostracizing me per my mother's request. Makes you wonder huh? This stuff was always on my mind at times like these while I am sitting up here in my bed trying to find some kind of peace via the word.

I would like to take this time and issue a warning to parents. Rearing a child is your God given responsibility. If he has blessed you with a precious gift, then it is your charge to bring them up in His statutes. Never allow frustration or misunderstanding to be the motivation for discipline. It's not just beating and yelling, but discipline involves teaching and training. It's a terrible thing to grow up unloved. I felt like an orphan. I often wondered was I left on their doorstep and they just felt sorry for me and kept me on. Nah…knowing those two they probably would have given me back to the state. That's just it they HAD to keep me, but sometimes, I wished to GOD they would have given me away.

Every day, my parents and I would argue. They would say things like lets concentrate on these other kids and forget about her. I wanted to be cosmetologist. I wanted to own my own shop and even create a skin care line for afro America sisters. That had been a dream of mine since I could remember. My first job was sweeping up hair in a barber shop at the age of 14. Lizzie Mae Thomas took pity on me and gave me my first shampoo gig at House of style on Court Street in my home town. From there, I went to vocational school to start the cosmetology trade. Yet my father wanted me to be an engineer. Engineer! I could barely add and he wanted me to have a career based on math?. What was he thinking? He asked me how would it look for him to have to tell his friends that he had a daughter learning how to do hair. This was probably after he had been bragging to everyone that I was in college.

I think the strategy was to break me down and make me see things their way. I got an "S" on my chest. I am a sagitarius to the max! There is no breaking one of us down! I will regroup and rebuild like that Terminator robot...only quicker! I was getting real tired of them putting me down. So I started to fight back. I wasn't twelve and scared anymore. I was grown, black and twenty-one. Yet they were still my mom and dad. The only parents I ever knew. Most evenings when my mom would walk in the house I would got o my room to avoid the barrage of yelling that came from her mouth. She was a miserable woman and she was not content unless everyone around her was nervous and in a tizzy. She did not have any real authority or influence so she did like white people in the Jim Crow era. She instilled fear. I would try to be asleep when she came home. My daily ritual included, sleeping until midnight. Then I would not have to deal with her and I could sit up all night to watch for death.

It could have been wishful thinking or the energy I felt coming from them, but I knew I wasn't long for this world. I was dying. I didn't know how or when, but I knew my time was short. I would spend days at a time planning my funeral and writing my eulogy. My best friend gave me a stereo and one of my mentors had given me the Winans 'Long Time Coming' album. This was a source of salvations for me.

***Secrets the Lord imparts***
***Keep them close to your heart***
***Don't ever let them die,***
***Make them the apple of your eye***

Those words got me from my 17th birthday to my 22nd. I once again had something to look forward to. I kept my dreams to myself. I held them hostage to my heart. I will no longer be a slave to small thinking. I began to dream big again. I wasn't holding those things in the right light though. I had years of put downs to out live. I had been told I was just going to end up with a house full of babies, shacked up with some drunk who beats me, waiting on my welfare check to come. Years of being insulted and criticized for being different were running me down. Instead of wanting to be better than average, I became bitter and blamed the scenery for my demise. I was so busy trying to prove everybody wrong that I forgot how to do right. My world was turned totally upside down. All my actions from that point on would be for vain glory.

I put my headphones on and started the record player. I was determined to find a word. As I flip through the worn pages, I land in the 12th chapter of Genesis. It read, "Get thee out from amongst thy kindred into a land I will show thee. Where you will be blessed and be a blessing. And those that bless you will be blessed and those that curse you will be cursed." That was like a balm to my aching soul, but where was I going to go who was going to help me? I know nothing and as my father once told me, I wasn't doing nothing but shitting and stepping in it. Unfortunately, he was right. At that time, everything I touched turned to ca-ca.

Even the church where I grew up, began to be a

source of tribulation. This was the cradle of my spirituality, where every summer I got saved to go back to school. They were not the most intelligent of the lot, but they did have a zealousness that most tried to mimic. I could see Mother Harris now with her little tom-tom drum, just banging and singing that whatever I needed God had. Sister Beatrice with her shrill nasally voice, banging on that piano off key and Sister Lvingston praying and jerking like she was having a seizure. The mother's board consisted of Mother Farris who would have you rolling with her sense of humor. Mother Butler, whose theme song was 'I saw the light' and she would do her little two step dance to top it off. The Bishop's wife, Mother Baker was the topper for them all. I could see her now standing to testify and thanking God for sanctifying her soul thru the truth, because His word was true anyhow! I can't help but chuckle at Brother Clayton, with his white hair and his wife Minnie, whose booty was so big she looked like a snail.

I often wondered why God would have me start off in such tacky surroundings. But this imagery fit my mother's persona. She puts you in the mind of that woman Stephen King portrayed on the movie Carrie. We listened to the kooky, whiney, white people's gospel channel on Sunday mornings instead of the jazzy black people radio station. I had to endure endless Saturday evenings listening to warbled voices of some white woman preacher. All of this made my mother feel saved. She would often poke

out her mouth and say ' I'm standing up for holiness', but she was knocking me down for spite. She was fanatical to a fault.

This bunch of weirdos made spirituality scary and almost science-fiction. They would say that God was punishing you by jerking you around and bouncing you like a rubber ball on the floor when you were disobedient. We had the oddest little bishop. He stood about 5'1, but with the size of his heart for us he as easily a giant. His favorite slogan was 'Don't mess wit' my chi'ren!' It was because of him that I was as involved as I was.

I had always been their scapegoat where someone else wouldn't I would. I based my whole life on what they said and what they thought of me. I lived to get their accolades and approval. After all that was my first impression of what spirituality was. If they were pleased then God must be. I taught Sunday school, I was in the junior and senior choirs, I directed them both, I was mistress of ceremonies and I was also a solo singer to fill in most of the young people programs. I even wrote and directed plays. I was in charge of bringing new songs to the choir as well as teaching all of the parts. To be honest, I had no idea what I was doing. I just could sing and so people naturally thought that was my passion. It was not. I had a yearning to usher. Just to be a door keeper in the house of the Lord. I wanted to be a junior usher so bad, that I lied to my mother who was the president of the usher board. How could I lie to my mother? You know, the one who birthed me into

this world. It was easy to do, she never paid any attention to me. Or even cared what was going on with me. She was too busy standing up for holiness.

All I wanted to do was go to church and be with my friends there. My mother was so mean to me that she took the only thing that I had going for me and tried to pervert it. She was busy standing up for holiness, but she was trying with all her strength to stamp out my spirituality. The reasoning behind this was the picture she had painted to everyone didn't match the real Susan. She would do things to keep me back, especially all the things that were church orientated that I wanted to do. Parents would kill to have a child like me. I loved everything church related. Every chance she got she would do things that would exclude me. I remember the day all of the youth were to be baptized. I was so excited until the Wednesday night service before it was to take place. I overheard her telling Aunt Gussy that I would just go down a dry devil and come up a wet one. What parent in their right mind would try to hold back a child that was seeking a higher calling? I had more highliter marks in her bible than she did. I rarely saw her reading God's word.

She and the other elders of the church had chosen my brother and that meant that there was none left for me. She tried with all her might to make him seem like an angel. If she only knew the devilment that boy was up to. Most of the things she would blame on me, he was responsible for doing. When I would try to explain she wouldn't hear any of it she would just start beating me. This somehow made her feel vindicated. Sometimes after she had whelted me up she would find out the truth, but it didn't matter she would just lie and say she whipped me because I had been disrespectful. In her narrow mind, me defending myself translated to disrespect. And then there were my two little sisters whom I did everything for except birth them into the world. I am only about 5 years older than my baby sisters, but I was a diaper changing, snotty nose whipping, bottle feeding frenzy. I believe my passion for doing hair came from me having to groom them. What little time I had left I would dedicate to my own grooming but it never was enough. I mean how much did a five year old know about immaculate hygiene. This coupled with the fact that I had a dark complexion, made me prime target for bullying. There were other kids at my church who smelt like pee and had dirty noses that used to ridicule me. To top all of this off my mother would burn my hair with those kiddi-kits. Man, she got me so good once that all my hair fell out and I had to wear a wig. Not the cute ones you see today, but hose old lady numbers with the long side burns and the knots in the back. Talk about humble beginnings.

Thank God for the place I called home, as much as she tried she could not stamp out my love for the church. I wanted to be there more than I wanted to be at home. I knew it to be a refuge even as a child. This was the only place I could go and be safe from the storm of my tiny life. Lately the Bishop's vision has been deterred. He is over eighty and in a rest home with his wife Jo. They were once the pinnacle of this community, but their replacement and his wife are living out their own vision. He is a simple minded farm boy who just loves to be the center of attention. He cannot preach, but he is very emotional. He cries like a little girl and people look over the fact that he has absolutely nothing to say. Missionary Perkins had recently asked me to fill in for her since she was not able to teach her Sunday school class. That conniving little imp saunters up to me and misquotes the scripture that says my gift and call would make room for me and said that there is no room for me there. They are going in a different direction. This was the final straw. Even my church was acing me out. I had nowhere else to turn to. Is it a wonder I got the heck away from them my first oppurtunity. I did not feel like I belonged or was even a part of that family. The home I grew up in, the school and church I attended all seemed so foreign to me now.

**The meeting...**

Two weeks had passed since I had the snake dream. Who was this mystery man that was going to diffuse the bomb my life had become. There were many revivals passing thru this country town. It was summer and most preachers saw our little town like the missionaries see the African continent.

I was headed to my little part time job one

Monday morning at our local mall. It housed three stores and the radio station that catered to rockers. As I was getting out of my car, I notice this small crowd of people milling about the mall entrance. A man who had on black pants, a white and those black/white shoes no one seems to know how to accessorize. The women had on jeans and I could not make out their faces, but they seemed so familiar to me. He jumps up from his seat and rushes towards me. I had stopped at the waffle house for a double pecan waffle and my hands were full. As I stand there juggling my purse and my breakfast, he approaches me with an extended hand and introduces himself. I try unsuccessfully to dodge but he yells out, "Hi my name is Apostle Miles and I'm with the Gospel of Life Deliverance ministries."

I manage to get everything in my left arm and stretch out my right hand to greet him. "Hi I am Susan Horton."

He counters with "Sister Horton, our car broke down and while we are stranded we are starting a revival and we were wondering if you could tell us who we need to contact to get the ball rolling."

I begin to rattle of different churches that they could start at an as ask if they needed any help. I listed mine because we are known for helping the sojourning saint. People often took advantage of us because we were the ones to lean on. I even offered to pass out fliers for them if they got me some copies. He thanked me and went back to their little group. I truly thought that was the last I would see of them.

I was in a church. Not my home church but this edifice belonged to Bethlehem CME. It was a dingy looking sanctuary that was paneled throughout the sanctuary and had a rickety old piano beside the pulpit. That guy that I just met was playing the piano and directing this small choir. I was an onlooker as well as singing in the little choir. It was an inaudible song but we were pouring our hearts into it. I wake up once again in a cold sweat. This is another burdensome day. The load here lately has not been as unbearable as usual. I can feel a change coming, I just don't know how or when.

By Wednesday, I get a visit from Shalisha. She was one of the women in Apostle Mile's entourage. We talk for a little about points of spirituality and pastoral welfare. I only spoke with her for a minute but I felt so much lighter. It may sound a little strange, but I felt a sisterly vibe pass between us. She gave me some more information about the revival that was to take place on Friday and the she left.

My boss at the time came out of the back room and asked who that was. I told her who she was and how I had met her. Bea felt it was her duty to protect me since she had become my confidante. I had confided in her thru all the turmoil I had been experiencing, and she had taken it upon herself to make some wrongs right. She owned the dress shop where I worked. Sometimes in lieu of pay, she would give me clothes. Since my parents wanted to control where I went and keep me on a short leash with their car, she gave her 2nd car so that I could get around.

She said she had a bad feeling about that woman. Bea and I had known each other for years. As a matter of fact I used to babysit her kids. She knew that I was not exaggerating about my family and that church. She left that same church because they ostracized her.

Friday was, here and I was as nervous as a new father to be. I did not know what to expect but I knew something was about to happen. As I am getting ready for the crusade, I tried to imagine how God was going to minister to me. What kind of word was he going to relay through the Apostle? As I prepare to depart, my mother starts an argument. Her efforts are futile. I was on my way to deliverance and there was nothing she could do to deter my change.

I arrive at the Ramada Inn 20 minutes early. I wanted to make sure that I got a good seat. As I get closer to the conference room, I feel as though I am walking closer to freedom. When I walk in the room, there were already two people in there. One of them was Reba, and the other was her sister, Jocelyn. The two ladies were totally different. I grew up under both of them. They were teenagers while I was still in grammar school. Their mother was a neighbor to my grandmother in the projects. I remember them from the block. Reba was a big jump rope fan, who was often seen playing hand jibe. Her sister was known for her sexual prowess. Jocelyn loved married men. A single man couldn't get the time of day from her. I walk up to them and speak. Jocelyn is extremely nervous for some reason. She asked me how

I was feeling. She then turns to me and says, "Girl ain't you scared?" Totally confused I ask her why. "Well Rae said he was a prophet." I had no idea what she was talking about. I knew her family was into voodoo and often consorted with spiritualists, so I just chalked it up to her strange upbringing.

The side door opened to the conference room opened and one of the ladies walked in. She was wearing a purple and green sweater dress. Her lingerie was failing because her nannies were sagging and the dress hung rather shabbily. Her complexion was that of a latte and she had dark lips. The next two ladies that came in were dressed a little better. One of them was caramel colored with a sort of tailored look about her and the 2nd woman was Shalisha. She was wearing a sand stone colored suit with sensible shoes and glasses. In walked Apostle Miles. The woman in the green and purple dress went over to him and began chatting away. By the way they were inter acting, I assumed that she was his wife. The last woman to enter from the side door came in and fell to her knees and began to pray. Apostle Miles walked out again, and the lady with the dark lips followed. I continued to greet some of the other guests that had arrived. I thought that there would be more people, but it was a nice size crowd. All of a sudden Apostle Miles rushes through the door up to the podium and begins to preach. He was speaking so fast I could barely keep up with what he was saying. He preached and ministered for about an hour, then be began to minister to people individually. By this time Jocelyn was about ready to run out of the room. He called out some woman who not familiar with and gave her a right now word about her finances. He then came over to Rae and wrapped his coat around her shoulders and asked her if she wanted that double portion of anointing that he had and she began praising GOD uncontrollably until she passed out. The other women were ministering too. They were quietly moving through the crowd laying hands and praying for people individually. I was anxiously awaiting my word. When is it going to be my turn?

Finally everything started to calm down and it was offering time. I had about fifteen dollars in my purse. As he gave a short ministry on giving, I emptied my pockets. I didn't mind giving at that time because I believed in that lie about God reciprocating what you gave to him. So I figured if I gave my all, there would be a word that would surpass my situation. At the end of the service we were all fellowshipping and I began a conversation with Nashi, the woman who came in and fell to her knees to pray. We talked about the service and general topics of spirituality. Soon after Shalisha runs up and grabs me around the neck. She hugs me as if we had been friends for years. Brittany, her sidekick, hugged me more out of obligatory greeting. The lady in the purple and green was walking around doing little odds and ends for the apostle. I later learned her name was Charlene.

As we stood around talking and laughing the

apostle came and sat across from us and joined our conversation. I said to him, "Boy you preached!" He just laughed. He then said to me "Would you like to come back with us?" I looked at the ladies and asked them was he serious and they all nodded a simultaneous yes. I stood there torn between joy and sheer terror. I didn't know the people from Adam's housecat. I had been packing all week but that was to move out of my parent's house into Bea's sister basement. I said sure I would go, but I would need a week to get my affairs in order. Isaac, the apostle, said that would be fine since he had to come back to the city anyway, he would just pick me up then. I was still standing there stunned and then Nashi grabbed me and hugged me. I just broke down and cried. That was the release I needed. As she hugged me, I could hear Brittany say, "You better do it Holyghost!"

***Saturday***

"What do you mean you movin' to Florida?" my mother was not too happy about the news. My father sat at the kitchen table pretending to read the news paper. That was his usual position when me and moma were going at it.

"You just met these people, you don't know nothing about 'em!" you need to go back to school a 'stead of runnin' behind a buncha strangers."

I was determined to make her see that she did not know what she was talking about. I got the same reaction from Bea when I told her the next day at work. She was disappointed that I was not moving with Pat her sister. Bea had made arrangements with her sister so that I could stay in my hometown without the hassles I was having with my parents every blessed day. She seemed to get more perturbed as the day went on. She repeatedly warned me that there was something strange about the whole thing. What did she know? I have finally started sleeping throughout the night again. God provided a way for me to escape and I was taking it. After I finished unpacking the new blouses and hanging them near the door, I bid Bea a good night. She warned me again and gave a hounds tooth printed suit. I thanked her she said, "No thanks needed. Just promise me that you will think about what I said. I know you feel like you ain't go now way out, but this ain't it."

On the drive home, I thought some more about Apostle Miles and the ladies. What was their life like, more importantly what would my life be like with them. Could this be the opportunity I had be praying so hard for? Or was it just another escape attempt. I was determined for it not to be the latter.

I thought about the last adventure that I went on. I moved to Oceanside, California to be with a member of our church whose husband got sent away to Bahrain. Marsha had heard that I had quit school and didn't have anything to do and thought it would be a good idea for me to come out to help with her 3 kids. I was out there for exactly five months. I cooked and cleaned, none of which pleased her. So I started looking for a job on the base. She took it personal and started sabotaging my efforts. If I needed a ride, she had something else to do. If I needed money, she didn't have any. When I was looking for a job in the city and I needed some help from the church that I joined while I was out there, she told them that she would pay me if I would continue to keep the kids. She failed to tell them that she had not paid me for the 3 months I had already kept them and she had offered very little support since I've been out there. She even started thinking I was stealing from her. Her mischievious children were misplacing things, even stealing food cause she never cooked and she blamed it on me. Her son Jason ate a whole bowl of cool whip and she accused me of stealing it. The only convincing evidence of my innocence was the empty container she found in their play area. I finally found a job at the PX. I was a grocery clerk until they transferred me to the hallmark store. There I worked for 2 months until I got into cosmetology school. I had enough to pay my tuition, and could even have worked a schedule to keep my hallmark job. As usual, I was not ready to make a step to better myself. I was more content complaining and wishing for a chance rather than getting prepared to take one.

Needless to say, I ran back to the cradle of confusion and restrictions. The first thing I did when I came home was shave my head. I always did that when things became unclear to me. It was like starting all over again. To prove I had control over something in my life I performed this self mutilation. This made my mother happy. She was accustomed to me looking like a pic-a-ninny. This made her feel better about herself somehow. She even made the comment, " Now you look like Susan." What exactly did "Susan" look like? When I left Cali I had gotten my ears pierced and my first hair weave. I was looking pretty cute. This new Susan looked well rested and ready for the world. Only thing is I had the old mentality. All of his weighing on my mind, I pull into the driveway and lay my head on the steering wheel. This week will prove to be the hardest I've had in a long time. Regardless of what anybody says or thinks, I am blowing this dirt water town.

***Sunday***

"He'll make a way…he'll make a way!" Reverend Robeson sang as he pointed to me during an altar call. I fake getting happy and pass out. I did not know what he was talking about, but it is always good to act out when they single you out, I mean I was already on their list no need to rock the boat. As it stands I had already made a mess of things by confiding in a person who I thought was on the up and up. Eula Harvis was an evangelist who attended our church and who was hell bent on revamping the way those country folk thought. She was known to question the motive of any one not exemplifying what was righteous.

For instance, when Mother Harris was talking about her husband who happened to be the Superintendent, and saying he was singing too much in Sunday school, she called her on it in front of the whole congregation. I needed someone like her to be an ally in my time of transition. But she was so busy trying to impress the current pastor. Not because she needed his approval, but she wanted them to implement some of the teachings she was availing herself to at the time. She in turn left me to the dogs. I know they didn't want me around because they saw **good** in me, they wanted me around to have someone to make to make them look good by comparison. She told the pastor and then proceeded to confer with him that it was a bad idea. I think he had a chip on his shoulder about the whole thing. He even told me if he had known that I was the 'Sister Horton" that Apostle Miles said told him to call he never would have helped them. He called me back to his study and basically told me that he thought that I was jumping the gun, he said that I was chasing rainbows and I needed to sit still and wait on God to make a way for me. I wanted to tell him he was a little too late to be concerned pastor now. I believe he was speaking out of professional jealousy. He thought he was the only man of God who cared about me. He told me he was going to check out this situation.

**Monday**

I began to pack up my room, deciding what to take and what to leave. When I went to California my mother offered me the pick of her closet. Now I barely had any clothes. The one or two pieces I had acquired were dry clean only so I took everything down to be cleaned. I didn't have a lot left to travel with. All I had left in the room was some albums, some books, pair of heels, a pair of Keds and a stereo. I was pairing my life down. Anything I didn't deem necessary to carry on this particular journey went into a box. So far I had packed up about 5 boxes. In case this turns out to be a dud too, I'll at least have packed up my things and prepared to get out of their house. I wanted to sit down and talk to my parents about this move and let them know why I felt I needed to do this. They had already teamed up with my pastor and were going to convince me to change my mind by Friday. I didn't want to leave my little sisters behind, but I needed to make this move for me. I needed space to grow. I needed to make a connection because I felt alone, so I called the only people in the world who were on my side. Charlene answered the phone. I heard kids in the back ground. In my mind I'm wondering where I was calling. I proceed to ask her some questions like how she was doing, and what was she doing. She told me she was watching the kids. I thought perhaps they are running a daycare. We chit and chat some more, and I hang up more confused than ever. No change ever comes easy.

**Tuesday**

I go in to talk to my boss and let her know that I was definitely going to Gainesville, Florida on Friday. When I finished my reasoning, all she could do was shake her head. She curtly asked me for the keys to her car and told me to get the rest of my things she didn't want me to come back. She even asked me for the clothes back that she had given me in lieu of pay. I told her they were in the cleansers. She waved her hand and said not to worry about it, just come on so she could drop me where ever. As she was taking me back to my parents, she warned me once again about trusting these strangers. There is something really strange about you just leaving and not knowing these people. Who was she to talk: she hired me to work in her store promising me 50.00 a day. That was highway robbery! I would be there 8-10 hours, hanging clothes, changing out merchandise, and helping her with the books. She paid me once and then she started giving me clothes, and when she started letting me use her car, she stopped even doing that. At that moment I knew then she was just using me, and now that her patsy was gone she would actually have to pay someone to do those things I was doing for free. I smile and bid her a final adieu; hopefully this will be the last time someone will use me.

**Wednesday**

I get to the sanctuary and the pastor calls me back to his study and proceeds to tell me that I have gotten mixed up with a bunch of crooks. They left a huge bill at the Ramada and did not pay. "They are not what you think they are so you should stay here!" I wanted to ask him what I was staying for. He himself had made it clear that there was no room for me there. I needed to know what other options I had. I told him that I still wanted to go. He said I needed to do something else besides chase rainbows. I pretty much tuned him out after that. My mind was in Florida, and as soon as I got home, I was going to call Isaac and see what this was all about.

Isaac explained to me that they had very little resources when they got stranded here, so they asked the hotel to credit everything and they would pay when they could. He said as soon as he saw Algae he was going to give him back that measly hundred dollars that they offered. He began to describe the station wagon that he thought algae drove that contained his homely wife and his dirty little kids. I laughed and corrected him. That was Deacon Bozeman, a portly man who looked like an over gown elf who spoke in a whisper and sang in a falsetto voice. As I said my good-byes, I reassured him that I would be ready Friday when he came. We confirmed the time and disconnected.

**Thursday**

I spent most of the day saying farewell to the people who were still talking to me.

**Friday**

WHEW!!! I made it. I could hardly sleep. I was nauseous and jittery. My mom still made one last attempt to keep me home. This temporary truce would have lasted only until the wee hours of the morning when she thought my opportunity to get away from them was gone, and then she would have resumed her bashing of my spirit.

He arrived about 4pm. I hadn't had a chance to finish putting my ducks all in a row. I still needed to get my clothes out of the cleaners. I was short of money. Bea didn't pay me for the last 3 days as she promised so I had to either ask my parents or …well if he doesn't then that means I can't go. That will be my final confirmation that I'm doing the right thing. When he got in the city, he called as promised. I was no good at giving directions, so I told him I would meet him at the mall where we first met. As I passed by the barber shop that housed my friend Cake, I waved my final good-bye…he waved a finger of regret at me. It didn't matter anymore, because I was shaking the dirt from this one horse town. Somehow I felt different about this time. I felt this world open up for the first time in a while.

"Hey are you ready to go?" He asked hurriedly. It was almost as if he was in a bigger hurry than me to shake the dust from this place.

"Not quite. See,…well I'm going to ask you to do something and if you do it then I'll know it was meant to be.

"What is it?" I don't know if it was the favor that annoyed him or if it was my attempt at being deep.

"Well I needed to get some clothes out of the cleaners and I don't have the money."

Without hesitation he answered, "Sure let's go."

As I was driving to Conscience cleaners in the heart of downtown, I heaved a sigh of relief. It was really happening. I had somewhere to go, somewhere to be…another chance at success. I felt as though I was drowning these past few months. You know when you've gone down for the last time and you just know that this is your last breathe. You dare to inhale, but there is no oxygen to fill your empty lungs. That's how I feel about my hometown. When I'm there I can't breathe. I can't sleep, nor can I think in a straight line. It could be from the negative energy that constantly surrounds me or it could be my personal hang up about living in a jar. It seems the people there have given up on having more. I'm not talking about *things* like material possessions, but experiences. I would love to see more cultural events where black people display an interest in something other than drinking and getting high. From the looks of the dope man's whip and his rags, they really want to escape the hum-drum life of the country. It seems their only extracurricular activities involve undermining each other and seeing who can bring you down he quickest.

"How much?" Apostle asked the clerk.

"It will be 40.00" the clerk accepted the bills from Apolstle's hand, and flipped the switch behind his back without looking. This activated that trolley that contained all the clothes. That was the final straw, Im outa here!!!!

"Rooosevelt my name." My dad stood and reached to shake the preacher's hand.

"Apostle Miles."

"Come on in...watch your step there...I'm still working on this place, and it's still got a lot things that need to be fixed." He pointed to a rickety old set of steps that adorned the front off a worn down Jim Walton home.

"Don't worry about your daughter. She's in good hands." Apostle Miles patted him on the shoulder and reassured him.

"Well she is a grown woman. Yeah I built that drive way myself. See I started on it a couple of years ago and I still haven't gotten the chance to finish it." His escapades with that old house were my dad's way of avoiding the matter at hand. If he had asked, I probably wouldn't have left.

That was always the case with my father and the house I grew up in. he wasn't a carpenter by trade, he was a barber and a truck driver. He ordered these orange and black books from the Time Life on do it yourself home repair and he learned how to pour cement, how to lay blocks and bricks, also how to frame houses. My father was real ingenuitive. He could build or fix anything…or tear it up trying. Our house has seen a lot of renovations in these past years. I believe my father sees that house as himself; always changing for the better. He has moved the kitchen where the bedrooms used to be; the dining room where the bathroom used to be and he bedrooms on the back porch…such is his life. He has gone from street urchin to a minister of God's living word. He is a misunderstood soul and knows exactly what I am going through. Seems like he would be an ally, but he can't it would look like he was taking sides. It's either me or my mother …yeah I know… and yes both are my natural parents, so it should be easy right?

As I go to my room for the last time, my mother and sister Sara come to help me get my things.

" He smell like doo-doo!" We all laugh. Whenever my mother wants to berate something she says it stinks or is ugly. In this case she was right, he smelt like a small child who did not wipe himself too good after a bm.

"Well I'm off family." I was so happy I could have

spit. I hug my mother and father for the last time and kiss my little sister. I look at my carry on and Sarah had slipped an orange from the counter and a pie she had been saving for herself in with my toiletries. I felt tears welling up in my eyes, but we don't show emotion. I look around to hug her, but displays of affection were not prominent in our family unit, so she took off running up the street. I call after her, "Come back here Sarah!" Humor is a way we deal with the surreal. Everyone laughs at the sight of us. After all is said and done, I get in that tan Toyota Celica and we head off to my new life in Gainesville, Florida.

## The Trip

"I know that the church has strayed, but there is no reason to give up on it." Isaac said matter factly.

"I just wish things would go back to a simpler time when we actually cared about a soul, and thought more of the parishioners than the offering!" I added.

"Yeah...God is in the process of bringing us back to where we once were. Look at you...it's no accident that we met! God has big plans for you and this ministry. I have seen some things about you, and you are a lot more than you believe you are and people will take notice to your ministry." He was always so good at motivating me.

I was totally full. I sit and look out the window. I was in between consciousness and unconsciousness. I was conscience of the fact that I had a ministry, but I was unconscious as to what it was. I was conscience that I was special, but unconscious as to how important I am to the body of Christ. I turn to look at Isaac and right before my eyes he was changing. He wasn't the way out I had ached for so long, but he was the angel of mercy God had sent to lead Lot out of Sodom and Gomorrah. I was happy for once and I let out a sigh of relief.

"Tell me some more about my new family!" My inquiry was that of an enthusiastic 5 year old.

"Well I am originally from Gainesville, Florida and Charlene is from Jamaica. Brittany, Shalisha, Nashi and Debbie are originally from Miami. All of them were students at UF. I used to be the musician for the gospel choir, then I became the chaplain and finally when I started this ministry, they were the only ones to follow me. I think the only one you haven't met ye is Debbie. By the way she is the assistant manager for a local convenience store there and she says you can have a job if you want it.

YESS!!! I had been wondering how I was going to earn a living, and God just keeps on making a way!

"I also need to tell you that Brittany and I have an eighteen month old son. Debbie and Nashi also have sons." He then looks at me to see if that made a difference. I wanted to say I grew up in a church where the chaste women of God were always popping up with these illegitimate children. Human fraility was no problem for me. I knew of many who had stood before the church to apologize for transgressing the Holy Ghost. Anyone can make a mistake it's what you do from then on that really counted. I made God a promise, that if he kept me, I would maintain my virginity until He sent m my husband. So far we were both holding up our promises to each other.

"Were you a student at UF?" I asked wanting to know more about him.

"No. I went to Morehouse in Atlanta, Ga." He said emphatically.

"What was your major?" I asked.

"Psychology. I was a doctor in Los Angeles, California. That's where I met Andre Crouch. I sang with him and his twin sister, Sandra God had given me a word for Andre, back then I was called Prophet

Miles. After I told him what God said, I turned and walked away. He called me back, and said most people who give me a word always want something in return. He asked me my name and if I could sing and rest is history. During the time I spent with their ministry I dated Gladys Knight."

"Wow!" I thought to myself, now I know why God had me to meet you all. Could it really be my time to shine? This man is connected in all kinds of ways. Then, as if her were reading my thoughts he says, "I know a lot of the large names in gospel."

He continues with, "Have you ever heard of James Moore?" I nodded yes.

"Well James and I go way back. He did a couple of workshops with the choir. Gary Wells, he is the director for Sounds of Blackness, also I met Twinkie Clarke when Andre's choir performed the opening for the Grammy's. We sang backup to ' I want to Know What Love Is'."

He was well connected. I couldn't wait to call home and spread the word about what I had found. I can't wait for those jokers to eat their hearts out!!!

My stomach interrupts our conversation with a small yelp.

"Do you want dinner? We could stop at one of these restaurants if you would like to.

I had not eaten all day. I was so excited about my exodus that I forgot to eat. I wasn't as hungry as I was anxious to get to my new home. I said, "Well I could wait til' we get home."

"Susan, I want to warn you about Gainesville. It is a wicked city and a principality sits over it."

I got a sinking feeling in the pit of my empty stomach. I had experiences with demons myself, but I had never known what the likes of a principality held in store. Not so long ago, I was asleep on one of those rare occasions and my spirit started to wrestle with something. As I struggled to say in the name of Jesus my spirit was screaming it but when I opened my mouth, it came out muffled and weak.

Finally whatever it was that was choking me started to slide off my bed, I could feel it moving to the floor and then I could open my eyes. I was afraid at the very mention of sprits or demons. That incident could have been nothing more than poor circulation, but how do you explain the entity I felt leaving my bed?

Demons have always frightened me, at least the way the church folk animated them to be these hideously deformed creatures that were sent by Satan to cause havoc and pain. There was another time in the church I grew up in where we were having a young people's program and the theme was 'It's Almost Midnight!'. Marsha, the woman who had tricked me out to California to babysit her bad kids, wrote it. It was one of those rare times when Al her husband was stationed somewhere she could not go, so she stayed in the city with her family. The subject was about being left behind after the rapture. We had rehearsed for weeks and practically had the whole city in the church. One particular woman had come.

She was known throughout the neighborhood as a loose woman. And she did not represent herself well at all. She had 2 daughters and one little boy. Her husband used to beat her and humiliate her at every waking moment. She tried to tell others of his abuse. But no one would believe her. She told my uncle that he used to stick his man part in her mouth when she was sleeping and choke her with it. He would also make her daughter's perform fellatio on him as well. Someone said she was just saying those things to get attention, because she was nuts. But I had been around enough to know when someone was telling the truth about some form of abuse or another. I don't believe she was crazy. I think she had a hard life she was trying to outlive and was not doing a successful job. Drugs, promiscuous sex and excessive behavior were her way of coping with a pain she had yet to let go.

Well as we began to perform the play we get to a scene where she starts to yell out and behave as though she wanted some attention. The elders in church knew that this was a spirit. The pastors recognized that this was not a dance of victory, but it looked ritualistic in nature. So he cuts off the music and she continues to dance out of control so he signals the ushers to cover her as she is starting to expose herself. She wallows and cries out so everything has to stop and notice her. She was writhing and moaning on the floor and she then starts to foam at the mouth. The mothers and pastors started to cast it out. Everyone was calling on the name of

Jesus. This spirit soon realizes that it was outnumbered and started to straighten up as if it had been cast out. The only thing that betrayed it was when Mother Harris asked her to say "Thank you Jesus". The woman acted as if she could not hear her and proceeded to fix her clothes as her breasts and panties were exposed.

Again Mother Harris asked her to say Jesus. That spirit shook its head and squinted as if to say you'd better watch our back. As the woman tried to leave the circle of prayer that they formed around her, each member was shouting at her in the name of Jesus. The woman began to spin out of control with her hands on her head covering her ears as if to say no, leave us alone. She got frustrated and ran for the back office as she was running out of the sanctuary we were told to stay put and pray out loud. As the mother and pastor followed her back there they found her on the hallway phone calling for someone to come and get her. She forgot that she was there with her children, she was just anxious to get away from that crazy church.

While she was talking to whoever was on the phone, the mother and pastor started laying hands on her again. She drops the phone and runs for the door but they stop her and began counseling her she appeared to be calmed enough to accompany them across the foyer to a Sunday school room. We got the word to resume the play but to make all our entrances from the back room. I notice the wife of the pastor, my mother and about two other members deep in thought. They were interceding for the situation in the foyer. They knew that spirit or spirits was still there and the mother and pastor were in danger.

As the play comes to an end, Val took her place in the choir stand and we begin singing the song Marsha wrote especially for the play. As Val is belting out the wrong words in her shaky monotone falsetto, there were cries from the audience. We thought it was the song, so in her best bad voice Val shuts her eyes and feigns a deep connection with what the spirit was doing. In spite of her cackling, there was something else going on. Mother Morgan later told me she heard that she heard that spirit cry out like a lion. When the pastor and Mother Harris came back they had this look on their faces that said we have seen something here tonight. They told us not only did she cry out like a lion, but her nails and teeth grew out. Now the mother and pastor could have collaborated their story, but how could Mother Morgan had known? Anyway needless to say the woman came out of the foyer looking completely different. She was a lot brighter and calmer. We looked at her and immediately began to dance for her deliverance. She was jumping and leaping saying I'm free. Then as things started to calm down Mother Harris gave her a warning that if she did not maintain her deliverance by staying in church and reading the word, those spirits would come back and bring seven more. Needless to say she came for a little while, but as with my old church, the ritualism's just are not enough. People are seeking a deeper connection with God and shouting and speaking in tongues are not enough to help you deal with real life. My knowledge of demonic forces is different now, as is my understanding of who is God now.

Isaac continues to warn me that his home town is wickedly run and that God had him there for a reason.

*My new home...*

As we pull into the garage, Nashi greets Isaac, and asks how you doing. I mistake her concern for him as concern for me, and I answer before he has a chance to.

"Oh I'm doing fine. Just happy to be home." I responded happily. Then I immediately felt uncomfortable like I had just pooted at the dinner table. I look up and both of them were smiling at me like my name was 'Lil Darryl'. She repeats the question and reaches over me to take his bag and close his car door. The two of them continue to talk as if I were not there. She asks if he had eaten and was there anything she could get him. I made a mental note in my mind that I needed to get used to how things were done. I also took notice to my new surroundings, if my friends could see me now. What a beautiful house. Inside the garage was another car, a black Grenada with brown frame and interior. They had named the car Freddie. The Toyota Celica that Isaac and I had been riding in was named "TC".

I later learned they named everything. As I walk into the house, there was a hallway with a guest bath and a door way that led to the kitchen. To the right was the den with a fireplace and adjacent was a closed in deck with the most breathe taking view of the woods. If only it were snowing. The house had an interesting layout. Just thru the kitchen was her dining room and directly connected to that was the master suite.

As we pass thru the den Nashi shows me the main bathroom, the boy's room, Brittany and Shalisha's room and finally her and Charlene's room. She shows me the upper hall closet that they prepared for me to store my things and while I was unpacking, she went back to the aide of Isaac. I could hear them whispering in the living room, and when I finished unpacking those 4 outfits I brought I went in to see what they were talking about. As I entered the room, I heard Nashi ask Isaac if he wanted something to drink and he asked if there was anything made and she retorted with the utmost enthusiasm that it was no problem to make him something. He barely noticed I was in the room until I open my mouth and say something totally irrelevant. Okay...I get it. I'm out of place in here. I have got to learn when to speak. He tells her to take me to the area I will be sleeping and before I could say anything else, she whisks me off to the den and shows me the pull out sofa.

"This is where you will be sleeping. Let me

show you how to set this up." She was hypnotically speaking.

"Oh, I know how to set up..." I began, but she interrupted me and proceeded to demonstrate this seemingly simple task.

"You take the pillows off the back, and lift them from the seat. You then grab this little tab and pull up not out. You want to watch your feet because those little legs drop pretty quickly. When your legs are stable, you want to fold down the bottom part. Then you make your bed like so."

I was amazed at how robotic this conversation was. It was almost like she was not talking to me. I took a mental note to mimic what I just saw. So this is how it was. I just stare at her to see what was really up, because I was a little frightened. She had a scar on her upper arm. It like someone had literally snatched flesh from her bone. She breaks my thought with a statement as if she had been reading my last few thoughts.

"When we are told to do something around here you do it heartily as unto the Lord. I am for one sold out and anything it takes to make the kingdom work, I'll do my best."

I thought to myself that I have got to get more serious. This was fantastic! I don't have that kind of dedication. I spent the rest of the conversation feeling like a novice. She was adamant about her service to the Lord. From there she began to tell me her story.

************************************************************

He called everyone around "Betsy" who was parked in the garage door with her hood up and a bent rod holding it up. We named all the cars. "TC" was the tan colored Toyota Celica. Betsy was a four door gremlin that looked exactly like her name; plain and goofy. She had puckered out before they could pull her in the driveway.

"How did this rod get bent?" He asked as if he already knew. I began to explain.

"I was letting down the garage door, when I heard Charlene screaming…" before I could finish the story, he interrupted.

"Of course you heard her screaming, she was probably telling you that you were tearing up the car! That was a real stupid spirit. You can't be going around doing dumb things like that!" He then grabs the basketball and tries to make a hoop. I was completely outdone. I had been locked up in this house for two straight months with 3 children who were not my own, no television, sleep deprived and barely any food. I was sick to my stomach literally and this guy proceeds to humiliate me…this is crazy. What did I have to go back to? Nothing and nobody.

I had alienated my family at his urging. He told me that the only way I was going to be free is to write a letter to my mother and tell her all the things that she had done to me. In the process of writing the letter I told her of some abuses that I had suffered at the hands of others. I pretty much blamed her for all the pain and anguish I had been experiencing thus far and that I never wanted to see them again. Simultaneously, she had sent me a fifty dollar money order and told me that I could come home any time I felt like it. Those two letters passed each other in the mail. When her letter to me arrived, I wanted to send it back to her, money order and all. Isaac had other plans for the cash. "Quick, hurry up and cash it before she changes her mind!" These were the words he said to Charlene. I was confused. I wanted nothing more to do with my parents at his unction and now he was taking money from them. I thought that was a bit cruel, but then I considered him to be a man of GOD so I did not question it.

That was the beginning of some sorrowful times for me. At the time I did not know it but I had jumped out of the frying pan and into the fire. I was being programmed and didn't know it. Being isolated and left alone was fostering the ideology that these people were the only ones who cared about me. The sleep deprivation and lack of food were the perfect distractions he needed to feed me weakened spiritual concepts and finally no contact to the outside world was like sensory deprivation. That house and all its contents became my world. I had lost all communication skills and my imagination had taken on a life of its own. Everyone around me was singing the same song. Nobody loved them and that we were all alone. Isaac became our mothers and fathers. He was teaching us things the local church had neglected and he was going to take us to the next spiritual level. I quickly succumbed to this propaganda and allowed this desolate place to become my spiritual home. I witnessed, I fasted, I studied and I even composed a few songs. I was going straight to the top and no one was going to stop me.

"Can I speak to Shalisha?" This was her younger sister Tyanna. I started to laugh. I had no idea where they were. I was left here daily with no concept of what was going on around me. In other words the only thing that had changed was my surroundings. I was still in the same place mentally that I had been in for the past 10 years. Nothing had changed about me. I thought when I severed the ties I had with my parents and all my old friends then things would be different. Not so.

"I honestly couldn't tell you where they are." I laughed again. Tyanna was a bit more somber than she usually is. I had met her before when Shalisha's mom came up for a visit. We made the pretense that everything was copacetic, and that Shalisha was not missing any of her studies. That was always strange to me. She and Nashi were allowed to proceed with their education. Dixie, Brittany, and Charlene worked, and I was locked in the house for days at time. But you don't give the mouse a chance to get free after he's been trapped.

"This ain't no *kee-kee!* Really, where is Shalisha?" This time she was a bit more insistant. Me being the silly ninny that I am, I answer her in the same way.

"Baby, I really couldn't tell you where they are." I continued to play with her repeating everything she says. My nonchalant answers coupled with Tyanna's need to stir up drama caused a big rift in the house relations. I didn't know it at the time, but I was exhibiting some serious signs of anxiety. I was breaking down and didn't know it. She hangs up the phone and I continue on with my daily chores. First I made the boys breakfast, then I would dress them and put them is Isaacs' room to watch one of their videos. As I stated before, Television had been outlawed in the house. The boys were the only ones who were allowed to watch it. He always made it a point to put them before us. I was supposed to be teaching them, but I had no idea how to do this so I would pray with them, read them a scripture and then let the videos do the rest. This was just some busy work to keep them occupied until I finished sweeping the house.

After the videos, it was lunch time. I fed them, cleaned them, and put them down for a nap. This gave me some time to study. This one particular time, Ishmael came home early from whatever it was he did during the daytime. He crept in from the side door and went directly to the kitchen. I saw his big black behind. I just chose to ignore him. He watched me for about five minutes and then walked thru the living room to try and surprise me.

I noticed him standing there out of my peripheral view, but I wanted to see what he was planning to do. I kept working as if he wasn't there. In my mind I knew he was trying to catch me doing something wrong so he could put me down in front of "them" again.

"Did anybody call here today?" He finally cleared his throat and asked.

"Yeah. I answered nonchalantly. "Just a call from Tyanna looking for Shalisha. I told her I didn't know where she was." I continued in a monotone voice. I was growing tired of these little interrogations that took place when something went wrong. They always talked to me like I was a child. True enough, I was the youngest of the group, but I was still an adult. They would make fun of me, and talk about how clumsy I was or my country slang or even the way I did things. To me, I was normal, but he even said I was nothing more than comic relief. This hurt me to the core, but I thought this was part of the next level training I was supposed to be getting so I allowed them to make light of me.

"Hmm... Ok." I knew this was the start of another put down session at my expense. I had been called stupid and dumb more times in their midst than in my whole life. I valued their opinion over my own, so I believed every negative comment they made about me. It turns out Tyanna, made a big mess out of me saying I couldn't tell her where Shalisha was. She told her mother that I was not allowed to tell her where Shalisha had gone. She had rallied all the other families and started an investigation into what we were doing.

Fortunately the children were the only ones getting good treatment at that time. They were next in line after Isaac. The order of authority went as follows: Isaac, the boys, and we got whatever was left over. Whenever he wanted to go out of town, or wanted a new suit, we were made to go without so he could have these things. He told us that ministry came before us. Our needs were not important when it came to his wants. I remember we were made to fast so that he could get his Mercedes out of the shop. I personally didn't even have a decent pair of underwear to change into, but I whenever I was working, I would faithfully sign over my checks to the ministry. That mentality soon trickled down to the boys. Charlene had to eventually start stealing money to buy shoes for the children he had fathered. We always seemed to be the target of some diabolical scheme to be over thrown.

At first I was intimidating to them because even in all the stuff they knew, my discernment and spiritual relationship was a little more advanced than theirs. To maintain that I was less than him or his students, Issaac would try to embarrass me, or put me down in their presence every chance he got. What he was afraid of was that my simple wit and real relationship with GOD would shine a light on his weak game and mess up his meal ticket. We were taking care of him. This was a spiritual version of the pimp/ho concept.

Defragmentation is the tool that weak men use to get into a woman's head. The insults and put downs were merely away to create a void in my self esteem. This gives him the fallow ground to plant whatever ideology he wanted and I would believe him. So many pastors use this same tool to keep parishioners subordinate to them. The member is made to believe that this simple man has more power than he actually has. He then will say things like he is your spiritual daddy to place himself in an authoritative role in your life.

Isaac claimed that GOD had called him to full-time ministry and we were to pool our resources together. When I was allowed to finally get a job, I would sign over my paychecks without even cashing them. I had dropped out of college and the best I could do was fast food restaurants or the occasional bookstore. This was working wonders on my self esteem. I had become so paranoid until I was thinking maybe I am less than the rest. They know so much and I know so little. So I better mimmick what I see them do until I grow a little more. We had these early morning bible studies that each of us took turns teaching. Then it was off to school or work for them and back to the babies and cleaning for me. Soon after the Tyanna incident, we lost the house and had to move into an extended stay hotel. Somehow this was my fault. I was the Jonah of the crew. Imagine 7 adults and 3 small children living in a single hotel room.

We were doing things like renting vans to go out of town and keeping them well past the return date. I remember that joker took us up to Tennessee for months on end trying to take over these white peoples church. It was an act of evangelism at first until he and the pastor of that assembly had words. They had made arrangements with two of the parishioners to provide a place to stay. Tim and Janice were their names. They had an 11 year old son that was very astute for his age. Tim and his wife were the perfect hosts for about 2 days. Nobody can stand house guests for too long...especially house guests that were of a different race and spirituality.

First of all she smoked and kept a dog in the house. This was not bad in and of itself, but they were sexual perverts. Tim had gotten his daughter pregnant and Janice had a crush on Isaac. Charlene, Brittany and me was the entourage he chose to stay up there with him. Or should I call us by our names at that time; Spineless, Bitchy, and Confused. Pure hell is the only way I could describe that time in Tennesee. I wanted to be back in that jail cell in Gainesville. Janice saw three black women and thought she had some live in maids, and Tim saw some extra booty to grab.

After the rift between us and them, we slept in the van until some old man named Mayfield eventually took pity on us and allowed us to sleep in his church. This man was not an orthodox Christian, he practiced voodoo. We had slid all the way down the charts on this one. He had all these statuettes of women that adorned his house. A house, by the way, that was totally disheveled. The atmosphere in that building was not one of spirituality but ritualism and control. I didn't know it at the time, but he had made arrangements to sell me to that old man for the lease of the building. Unfortunately for him, I am not the bartering type. I honestly believed in ministry and that all the suffering we were doing was necessary to get to the good stuff. I had placed this man over my own father and given him such place in my life until, I could see the scandals and would not react to any of it.

Coincidentally there was another woman with whom he had to have a "private" counsel with. She developed an obsession with him as did all the others. I am the type that saw cracks in the stories he told us and would call him on his crap, but he knew how to flip the script and make it seem like I am the weak link. In an attempt to maintain control he would belittle my intuition, criticize my spiritual discernment, and berate my ability. He put me down so bad until I wanted to die. This was the final nail in my coffin. I even believed that I was just too stupid to live. All of the turmoil we were experiencing was my fault. I couldn't do anything right so I decided to stay under the radar and accept my lot as a dumb beast of burden. I even started to doubt my own discernment and spiritual logic. This drove the point home that we were in some next level ministry.

Gainesville was Isaac's hometown, so he had foreknowledge of all the local churches that we never got to visit, but were somehow targeted by them all. It turns out that he had caused quite a raucus in his past and made quite a few enemies. It never dawned on me that we never went to church, nor did we have our own services, but we were calling ourselves a ministry.

I suffered from depression even then. I would get

in these moods where I could not for the life of me tell you what was wrong with me. I felt as though I was in hole, buried under an iron apron and there was very little oxygen. I was in a hopeless state of mind and everyone thought it was their duty to bring me out of it. "Get over it" became a constant rebuke that the others snarled at me. I didn't know how. How do you turn off a thunderstorm? You can't. You just have to let it rain. I was sad, but not enough to cry. I was in pain, but I couldn't pin point exactly where I was hurting. These times have been happening to me since I was a little girl. I walked around with this pained look on my face. All of them thought it was to get attention, but that was how I was feeling.

There was a chain of command in the midst of the females. Charlene was the "pastor". She was a chemistry major whose parents were wealthy and lived in Dakkar, Senegal. Brittany was next in command and also a prophetess. Her family's claim to fame was that her sister was a rock star, and had it not been with for her involvement with Isaac, she would have been the perfect snob. Shalisha was once in the position that Charlene had, but now she was third in command. Her mother was supervisor at Fed-Ex.

Then there was Debbie, she had the calmest demeanor of us all. She never really talked about her familial ties. After all of them was Nashi and myself. Nashi was a ding-bat who made herself seem more than what she was. Her family did have a little bit of money, but she was so busy trying to make a name for herself that she didn't allow it to deter her from becoming this great woman of GOD. All of them came from upper to middle class families that had a little bit of money. Me, I was just this poor, undereducated, swamp running pic-a ninny who had no idea what was going on in the world. I was still dreaming of becoming a gospel star. Not because, I wanted to be a minister of music, nor to elevate the kingdom of GOD, but because I wanted to prove my parents and everyone else wrong. I wanted them to envy me. I wanted to rub all their faces in it.

In this hierarchy was Ishmael's involvement with each woman. During our brief involvements with other churches, there was the occasional affair. Like in Tennesee, there was Pat who got pregnant for him and another woman he was trying to influence to move Gainseville. To add to this long list of affairs there was Barbara in Ocala, Timesha in Jacksonville, and Deloris in Americus. I had no idea he had been sleeping with these women, until Brittany got pregnant, and Dixie totally lost it. I had come home one day and caught him and Dixie in the back bedroom, while the boys were in the living room. I didn't think anything of it until she too came up pregnant. By this time, I was so gone in the mind that I was afraid to believe my own eyes. So I questioned him. He told me that Brittany was trying to trap him and that Dixie was just hysterical for no reason. This made me really doubt him as a man of God.

There had been other instances like when he read my notebook from Alabama State University and called out some random names I had written on the top of the folder. Those names had been written on there because before I left my hometown, I was planning a workshop. He was fishing and it was obvious. He said that Reggie a bass singer was coming to Florida and that I needed to be able to handle it. He also told me that I needed to stop thinking with my crotch, when I gave Paul Barksdale our number. Paul was a guy that I knew from the ASU gospel choir and he was the only familiar face I had seen since I had been down here in this GOD-forsaken town. I thought to myself, why couldn't he contact me? My crotch wasn't an issue because it was common knowledge that Paul was an undercover sissy. Most of the men who attended ASU had some dealings with other men. They didn't knick-name it "All Sissy University" for nothing. This was just one more way he chose to humiliate me. I was the only virgin of the crew, but because I was honest about my feelings I was called a whore. We weren't allowed to have boyfriends or even to date. It interfered with ministry. I didn't bother to tell him this because what he "wasn't" was becoming painfully clear. Men were a distraction as he would say.

This is also another characteristic of an occult. Interactions with the opposite sex by the members was frowned upon, even though the leader has multiple relationships. In so many of our churches today, the only people getting married is the minister's daughters or sons. If you can't remember the last wedding that took place in your local assembly, you might want to check out your leadership.

This domineering man had control over all of our minds. I couldn't call him on it then, because that would mean that I was wrong again. I had to hold this illusion together. This was my last chance. He had gone through my personal things and read information and then pretended that GOD had given him special instructions regarding me. I really wanted to call him on his mess, but again, this would mean that I had made another irrational decision. I had begun to be sick all the time. I would vomit for days at the mere mention of food. I thought that GOD was punishing me. This was another tool he used to control us. He would tell us that to contact our families would bring harm and death to us if we chose them over the ministry. I knew that I was the worst of the lot, but he had influenced me to believe that only those things happened when GOD was angry with someone. I later learned that I had developed gall stones, but since I was one of the lesser ones, my sickness didn't matter. My parents were not wealthy, nor did I have a job that provided insurance, so I was told to pray for myself and keep it moving.

There were instances where I would lock myself in the bathroom and just pray and cry for GOD to help me to understand what was going on with me. Every morning at around 3 am I would get up, grab Shalisha's NIV bible and head the bathroom. That was the only room in the hotel where we could have some privacy. Sitting on the side of the tub and crying out to God was the only release that I had. We always talked about ministry, but never went to any churches. Whenever we did, we got put out for some sort of scandal.

There was Daniel, his spiritual brother. They had grown up together and had done lots of dirt in their past relationship. He had agreed to become a part of our ministry. That tie was severed when Ishmael got caught in the bed with one of his choir members. There was the church in Jacksonville, Fla that got wind of his antics after one of the members came forth about the affair she had with him. He had also stolen some camera equipment from one of the members there, but of course we heard a different story. There was Americus, Georgia where he went with one of the ministers wives and so on. We have been booted out of more churches than the law should allow. All of these things should have made us see that what we were doing was not of God, but some outcast's imagination. We were willing participants in this sadist's game of spiritual conquest.

As a result of my 3am prayer sessions, I began to grow stronger. My thirst for God's word became insatiable. I was studying day and night. I did not know that God was preparing my exodus. It happened in the strangest way.

One day we were performing our usual household duties and it just occurred to me that I didn't want to be there anymore. I felt mistreated and dirty. I felt as if I had been choking and couldn't find the strength to cough. We had been to the laundry mat.

I felt my freedom at hand, but instead of rejoicing, I was saddened and irritated. I spent the entire day in a blue fog. I didn't know it was good bye, but when we arrived back at the hotel we were living in, I knew. We had specific instructions for lunch that day, but I chose to eat the leftovers that were in the refrigerator. Brittany who needed to be in control came into the kitchen to start an argument…not necessarily I would just lay down and take whatever they said, but not today. I quickly retorted that this food had been in the refrigerator too long and was going be thrown away anyway so why not. She ran down the hall to the only bedroom we had to snitch to Isaac. She always did this when she couldn't get her way. Mind you they had two children together under the guise of doing the Lord's work. So she wasn't just his right hand prophetess, she was his mistress. She used this as a platform to manipulate her way. He called me in the room and when he did that, all of the 3 years I spent in that hell hole come pouring out like vomit. I told him that I didn't trust him and that I do not believe in what was he was doing. I had had it with this farse of a ministry and I wanted to leave. That is when he went proactive and proceeds to put me out. He called Nashi who was the treasurer at the time and told her to see how much they needed to get me a bus ticket back to Prattville.

One night, I had a dream. This was the beginning of the end for me.

*...but I really do love the Lord!!!*

Excuse me please. Allow me to come down off the cross for just a moment. I know somebody out there needs the wood, so I must speak out of an enlightened spirit for the next few pages. There is some soul who is reading this and is caught up in the same garbage that I was. It may not be a pimp style preacher or even an overbearing religious figure in your life that has you bound. Matter of fact, it's not. It is you!

Listen to me like you have never listened to anyone before. It is your own need to be heard that has stifled your inner voice. Your desire to be better than average has caused you to judge the rest, and that has crippled you. It's even that need to be more spiritual that has made you a type of leper. It seems like the closer you get to your human goals, the further GOD pulls you away. Since your ears have become heavy, allow me to re iterate...STOP THINKING LIKE A HUMAN!

Recently I met a young lady who has been in church for years. If you were to have a conversation with her, you could feel the anointing just listening to her profess and declare God's promises. Keep listening to her and the words become bitter and tangled with self defeat and judgement towards others. She will tell you how God gave her a vision for health care and then she will continue to tell you how she got in cahoots with a crooked preacher to get grants from the government so she could start the business. Go a little further and she will inform you how the preacher scammed her out of thousands and she is now homeless and spiritually confused because she has to pay it all back. Those promises are yet to be fulfilled because she gave her vision to a crook. Now the vines from that fettered "spiritual father/ daughter" relationship is choking the spiritual life out of her.

You are already the person you are trying to become. Before I grasped this concept, GOD pulled my coat tail one day when I was stressing over minor details of my life and HE told me that I was living a poor imitation of myself. I was so busy trying to "be" until I never really got around to actually being. I had this image in my head that I wanted to project, but it kept coming out wrong. I wanted to be good, but I would end up being bad. I wanted to look sweet and caring, but I ended up being overbearing and selfish. I wanted to project the image of a humorously enlightened pillar, but instead I was just a rock. All of the things I tried to "be", when I wasn't looking I WAS. If I had known how to just be still in my mind, cast down those imaginary audiences I was performing for, and relax into my own character, I would not have had the privilege to be writing this book for your instruction. My life is a message of what not to do. I played around in school, being the buffoon for my classmates while they were working their butts off to get into college. When I went to college, I was looking for my prince to rescue me from this humdrum existence. When I got out on my own I was trying to replicate the torment that I grew up with, but with better props. I spent the last 39 years of my life in a fog.

You remember when you were trying to learn how to swim and during the lessons you fell into the pool. You struggled to get your bearings, and you really didn't know which way was up. That's the fog that I have been walking around in. I have literally been turned upside down. That is the precipice for all the negative and tumultuous decisions I have made. That sister is living in the same fog. She, just as I had, has a mind full of spiritual litter. She is scattered and shook so that she can't be reached. The only difference between she and I is I am taking responsibility for my contribution to my own demise. Nobody and everybody is responsible for my stuck in the mud persona. I haven't been able to see myself anywhere else but following someone else. I wasn't a trend setter, or a go getter I was just stuck.

As I sit here and think about some of the times I could have stood up for myself but I let someone else have my esteem, I feel vindicated. Not because I am blaming someone else, but I can see the error in my ways and am now able to choose and speak up for myself. I am no longer the victim but the victor.

Isaac and the next joker I am about to introduce you to are prime examples of what's going on in our church's today. After they threw me out of GOLDM, I was afraid for my life. I was told, no it was insinuated, that if I left I was a dead woman. It was all in my head. In my mind there had been established this boundary. See whenever one of us tried to make contact with our families or they tried to contact us or we even tried to come outside of this hell Isaac had laid out for us, we were punished. A few misguided quotes and prophecies and in my mind there was an electrical fence I could not cross. I really believed that this man held my fate.

I remember the dream I had the week before I left. We were running. Myself and all the ladies that had become a part of this ministry, we were running towards this dilapidated little house. The wood was old and worn. There were weeds and dying vines growing all through the framework. One of the girls, who was pregnant at the time, had had her baby. He looked just like Isaac. He had on a blue and white checkered romper and he had long hair. His hair had plaited to look like a girl and there were barrettes on the ends even though he was a little boy. Now this was not unusual, because the one who was his mother had been warned that she was going to make her other son weak if she didn't stop coddling him. When we arrived at this house, it turned out to be a church. We had on our singing uniforms which were these black and gold suits. Mine was different, because I was not an original member of the group. Also the suit I wore was different in that it was not only my gold/black suit it was also half my favorite white suit. As we walked into this church, it was very familiar to me…as a matter of fact it was just like the church I grew up in. In the choir stand there were all these people who were light skinned and had big noses. They all resembled each other. I got up to go to the bathroom and there I saw that my gold and black suit side had been soiled, so I took it off and threw it on the pile with the others that were covering the bathroom floor.

Approximately a month to the day, I was arriving at the next cult. The pastor of this church was light skinned and had a big nose and all of the members acted like him in some way or another, also, this edifice looked exactly like the church I grew up in. This man was like all the rest, a lying, conniving, shifty, underhanded, snake in the grass that stole money in the name of the Lord and caused many to stumble. He slept with his female associate pastors and even one of his associate pastor's wives. This demon even molested some of the church's youth. I saw him make a pass at a woman in a Piccadilly restaurant by sending one of his nurses over with his business cards. He had a best friend who later came out of the closet, with whom he did a lot of out of town travel (you saw Brokeback Mountain) and whom he claims he did not know was homosexual, but he would brag about how keen his discernment was. He went to seminars conducted by Reverend Ike and there was this sissy who attended with him. He would come back from these out of town exploits all refreshed and climb into the pulpit wearing finger waves and knee-hi stockings. He was doing all of this while he was tearing down and insulting his parishioners and steadily shaking them down for more money.

The perversions he tried to conceal trickled down

thru his family. He had openly gay or cross dressing brothers. Even his brother that he made "Head Deacon", got fired from his job for making a man suck his penis. It didn't stop with that generation it even began to show in their children. His daughter would stand up amidst the congregation and brag about her virtue and later it was discovered that she had contradicted herpes from sleeping with somebody's husband. This deacon's son, whom he had been calling a preacher, got hooked on crack and has spent several years in prison for drug trafficking.

See these so called "men of God" are just men. They lie, cheat, steal, belittle, manipulate, connive and stir up dissension in the ranks all in an effort to keep the flock scattered just enough to get money. That's what all this is about, money. Myself and people like me are the pawns that they cast to the side to keep the money flowing. They may give us great swelling prophecies about how special we are to the body of Christ and that there is a special reward waiting for us if we could just arrive at this particular place in God. Let's herein refer to it as a spiritual Atlantis...nobody knows exactly where this place is and how to get there.

While we are journeying to this imaginary place, there are many foul ups and we are encouraged to keep trying one day we will make it. All the while we are traveling, we are encouraged to give and it will one day it will be us on the receiving end. During this painful expedition of ours, there are a few that have been placed above the control group and these are the ones that have made it to that level. They are flaunted and deemed mo' better than the rest of us. What these fantastic people are is the one who is close to the situation, you know like the wife, the daughter/son, the aunt or uncle or undercover lover. These people have a stake in this con so they play the humble roll to keep taking your and my money. They are usually more messed up than this preacher that has made himself the head of this pyramid.

Now let me remind you, Jesus is the shepherd. Not a man. He has not given your soul to anybody for safe keeping. I heard one of these silly preachers tell me that I needed to be under a covering. It was completely laughable. I stood there and looked at him with his perfectly manicured, French tipped, egg shaped nails and shiny lips, and thought to myself, brother I don't want to be as covered as you. He was practically buried! All souls are mine sayeth the Lord, but the soul that sinneth it shall die. Again, nobody knows what these sins actually are. They will tell you its alcohol, smoking weed, sex, gambling, clubbing, hanging out with your friends, going to the movies, dances, social gatherings, etc., but none of these were mentioned in the Ten Commandments.

This is all part of the con. To get you struggling with things that are fun to do and create a conviction about things that are given to your nature. Once they get you arguing with your body and using your own mind to create this oasis that you have got to stamp out your humanness to get to, your are totally confused, and ripe for the taking . While you're struggling to kill yourself and to deny the very things that make you who you are, they are robbing you blind!

This is making perfect sense to some of you, but get this, he has already told you that the devil is going to tell you he is stealing from you, so who are you going to listen to him or me? I'm not taking anything from you, this is seed. You are blessing me, because I am the covering for your soul. The word says if you give a prophet a glass of water you will receive a prophet's reward...what exactly is that? A glass of water perhaps? We are giving all of our precious belongings to someone in order to get more belongings. That is why the con is so successful, they are selling us greed!

Isn't that silly? You already have what you are giving away! You are already confused and don't know which way the bubbles are flowing so you are going to go with the one he(anti-christ) already told you to listen to in the first place. Madness isn't it? He( the anti-christ) has created this wicked force for you to rebel against. The definition for "anti" is simply opposite. Christ came that we may have life and one that is more abundant, but you are being encouraged to live a life that is squandered and lacking in every way. Now in our feeble minds everything that goes against what he(the anti-christ) has taught us is of the enemy...or the devil, which we are in an imaginary war with. Even if it is your own family you will sacrifice them for the benefit of advancing towards your Atlantis. He (the anti-christ) will down play and encourage you to forget about obeying the Ten Commandments. Now those are the only laws we should be worried about breaking. All of these other rituals are a way to keep you wondering and confused. We have been rebuked for simple human propensities. We are tripping over the fact that we cannot live up to some imaginary standard set forth by a man who cannot live up to it himself. We could give all of this connery to the credit of a few greedy preachers, but it wasn't their idea. Man's weakness was the whole purpose of Calvary. Adam could not take responsibility for his own contribution to Eve's demise so God took it for him.

Pawns. We have been living our lives as pawns. It's time now that we stand up and take back our natural authority. We are the church. We have already arrived and live everyday in our Atlantis. We are the powers we are so diligently trying to possess. ***We are.***

Recently I had the privilege of fellowshipping with another church. During my participation there, I was told that it was time to become a licensed minister. The co-pastor stood in the midst of the congregation and began to prophesy that it was now time for me to take the pulpit. She said that I should write the vision for my program and that I should call my family, and let all my acquaintenances know that they should come and celebrate with me. I was excited, because that has been a goal of mine since I accepted the call. I did as instructed and set the date and began to plan the program. Even as she was speaking, I felt unworthy and unsure. I didn't see how my understanding up to that point would fit into the traditional form of what we know as "church". I did not believe in speaking in tongues, or laying on of hands...at least not in the same context as most who practice these rituals. I still believed that you could drink alcohol, smoke and even got to clubs and enjoy what they call secular music. Per my understanding and relationship with GOD, the only sin is unforgiveness. HE even gave me revelation that said only the soul could sin. The flesh is faulty from the word go and salvation was not intended to cover any deeds it does, but salvation was a reconnecting to the spirit of God.

More importantly, I did not believe in giving ten percent of my earnings to, what they called the "storehouse". Let's look at the concept of tithing shall we. Joseph(Genesis 40:1-42) was given a revelation via the Pharoah's dream of how to preserve the population during a time of famine. Each household was to bring a percentage of their crop yields to a communal trust and ensure the survival of each family during the time of a seven year drought. When you bring something to be stored, you can usually go back and utilize it. This concept was taken a step further by the Levites(Leviticus 18:1-32 & Deut: 26) to ensure their survival during the time of the exodus.

Tithes were not to be given but once a year, when **ALL** of a man's household including his children and servants, was accounted for and it was only during the harvest that ten percent of the crops or livestock were to be given to the Levites. By bringing these offerings to the Lord via the priesthood, the 12 tribes of Israel were also making atonement for their transgressions. If it was an acceptable sacrifice, then the priests were spared. When the priest didn't return, then the people knew that their sin was unaccounted for. It may not have been the fact the people's sin was too great for the fat of rams; it may have been that the priest himself was unworthy to bring such a gift before Jehovah. This my friends is why that erroneous message about us needing a covering has no validity. You do not need to go to church to be covered by GOD's grace. We already tried to use man as a covering and we were left wanting. GOD grew tired of these half hearted attempts at salvation. The word says the stench of this burning of unacceptable sacrifice had reached heaven and it made GOD penitent that he had made man. So to ensure that we were never again left to our own spiritual devices, He spoke out a part of himself (Jesus, the Christ) and offered Himself up. My friends when we are told and believe the lie that we need a man to do what Jesus has already done, we are crucifying him afresh. If it was in man's ability to do, Adam could have saved Eve, Lot could have saved Sodom and Gomorrah, and Moses could have gone into Canaan. People it is **NOT** possible for us to undo what has already been done. No sin can come between the Father and us...except the sin of **unforgiveness**. Now all we need to do is accept His extension of grace. It's like showing up at the finest restaurant and finding out that whatever your appetite or propensity, your bill is *gratis*.

Now if there was ever an exception to this understanding, it was this set of people. I had received more support from them in the past 3 months than I had received from my family in the whole 40 years that I have been alive. They brought food to my house, they gave me gas money, they even went with me to doctors appointments, but I was not buying into the hype. No one does anything in this life without an agenda.

Needless to say, the date I was instructed to seek GOD for, came and went and I am still unlicensed. Their intentions were to have me jumping thru hoops and running in place while they dangle that carrot of a license, to do what I have been doing all along, before me. One day while I was anguishing over the hospitality committee, the altar guild, the ministry as a whole, GOD spoke to me via my relationship with His voice and said "LET THAT GO!" When He spoke those words into my spirit, the peace that surpassed my understanding to that point washed over me and I was once again free. I haven't looked back since. I have to wonder what HE wanted me to learn from this little event. As a result of my intermingling with this particular sect, I have gained a better understanding about who I am as a Christian and some clarity about what I want as a minister. I refuse to live in a shell and wait for the rapture, only fellowshipping with people who believe like I do.

While we are busy trying to impress each other

with how sanctimonious we are, life is passing us by. I don't want to confine my experiences only to a narrow minded set of people. This is a basis for occultism. I have been down this road before. They had set me up like so many of the others before them. They prophesied many blessings and riches and even businesses. Not that there was anything wrong with this, because this is something GOD had already shared with me. I had a heart scare, but where was the warning for this? I was told that I was going to be smiling a lot more, but why didn't they tell me that tears were the forerunner for this fortune. He even predicted that Boaz was on the way. Now this is a "biggie" when it comes to single Christian women. Most…,some…,naw…, a **few** of us are still holding on to our virtue and are waiting desperately to be on the other side of physical want. I have news for you my sisters, even when you cross that threshold of marriage, a restless nature will not be a thing of the past.

I shared this experience with you before God gave me another understanding. Superstition is the basis for the modern day church and its practices now. Most of the beliefs we hold dear to our little twisted hearts, are a direct result of voodoo practices and old wives tales. The basis for superstition and voodoo is fear. Look at how these silly preachers are controlling you and keeping you confined to a building by telling you that if you leave me, you won't be covered by grace anymore. They are cursing our finances and telling us that we will continue to sink in the quicksand of debt if we don't give our monies to them or the ever popular, you aren't mature enough yet, keep working out your soul salvation. All of these lies are told to us to keep us in the yard of the church. These half truths are like invisible leashes to keep us paying monies, giving away our gifts and talents and depending on some man to provide us with the spiritual validity Jesus died for.

No one has the ability to curse or bless you! What door can man shut that GOD has opened? As a man thinketh in his heart, so is he. If you believe that you are cursed then everything about you will perform in a cursed manor. I have seen this impish man stand in the pulpit at a funeral and brag about how God had given him the power to raise the dead, but under the circumstances it wouldn't be wise to do so. I'm sorry, but I have had it with these lying wonders pretending that they have all of this authority and they don't have enough power to blow dust off of a peanut. We, like the chumps we are, fall for it hook, line, and sinker.

The incident of demon possession, that I had the great fortune to witness early on in my fellowship with Christ, was an extreme demonstration of emotionalism. This woman had real issues and through the instigation of the church leaders, she was acting them out. They were giving her cues as to how she should behave. When she was dancing and acting wild, they were shouting at her and causing her to become even more aniamted. When she started wallowing on the floor, they were telling her to cry out and let it go. It's amazing how she calmed down enough to make a phone call. Again family, some things are not the devil, but just devilish of us to do. I have made all of these observations and poured before God just to tell you to stand still and see the salvation of the Lord.